FULL PARDON

A Message of Hope

Bible verses
All Scripture quotations are taken from the
Holy Bible, New International Version.
© Copyright 1973, 1978, 1984.
Used by permission of International Bible Society.
All rights reserved.

Additional text
Richard Coss
© 1984 Bible League International
Revised edition © 2006

Published by

Bible League®
I N T E R N A T I O N A L

P.O. Box 28000, Chicago, IL 60628, USA

www.BibleLeague.org

800-871-5445

─────

This resource is also available from these Bible League International office locations:

P.O. Box 714, Penrith, NSW 2751, Australia (1800-800-937)
P.O. Box 21246, Henderson, Waitakere 0650, New Zealand (+9-836-1643)

Printed in USA   A100–0021

About the author...

Richard Coss began his life of crime at the young age of 9. By the time he was 25, he had spent 10 years locked up behind bars. Hi s rap sheet included 32 arrests and 28 convictions. At the time, the FBI described him as dangerous and incorrigible.

Coss heard the Good News of Jesus Christ during his third and final stint in prison. And God's Word transformed his life. On March 16, 1969, as a 25-year-old inmate in El Reno Federal Reformatory in Oklahoma, he gave his life to Jesus Christ. Less than 19 months later, on November 12, 1970, he received a parole from prison. Gerald R. Ford granted him a Presidential Pardon on December 23, 1975.

Since then, Coss has served His Lord and Savior as an evangelist, sharing the life-saving Word of God to prisons, churches, youth groups, jails, and more. Coss has directed Christ Bars None prison ministries (www.ChristBarsNone.com) since 1976.

Hope is like
 a beautiful flower
 that grows
 even when
 everything else
 seems bleak and dark
 and hopeless.
Put your hope
 in God!
Read this booklet
 and learn
 how God is able
 and willing
 to grant you
 a full pardon!

God understands ─────────

God knows all about you.
>He has access to the
>>Real You
>that no one else
>>can see
>>or know
>unless you let him.

God knows you.
He knows your heart.
He understands your
>hurts and disappointments,
>your fears and apprehensions.

He knows how you
>struggle
>in bondage to sin, and
>He understands.

He can be your most intimate friend.
>Talk to Him.
>Listen to Him.

He really does understand!

The Bible says . . .

Cast all your anxiety on him [God],
    because he cares
        for you.

1 Peter 5:7

No temptation has seized you
    except what is common to man.
And God is faithful;
    he will not let you be tempted
    beyond what you can bear.
But when you are tempted,
    he will also provide a way out
    so that you can stand up under it.

1 Corinthians 10:13

God said,
    "Call to me and
        I will answer you
    and tell you great
        and unsearchable things
    you do not know."

Jeremiah 33:3

What, then, shall we say
    in response to this?
If God is for us,
    who can be against us?

Romans 8:31

Discouragement ———

When you become disheartened
    and discouraged,
and you need to talk to someone
    who really understands
    what you are going through,
        talk to the Lord!

He has been there.

He knows exactly
    what you are feeling.

Jesus was arrested,
    tried,
        convicted,
            and executed.

He was mocked,
    humiliated,
        and beaten
            as He was run through
                The System.

He understands as no other.

You can trust Him
    with your true feelings.

Talk to Him!

The Bible says . . .

We are hard pressed on every side,
*   but not crushed;*
*   perplexed, but not in despair;*
*   persecuted, but not abandoned;*
*   struck down, but not destroyed.*
                    2 Corinthians 4:8–9

Though I walk in the midst of trouble,
*   you [God] preserve my life;*
you stretch out your hand
*   against the anger of my foes,*
with your right hand
*   you save me.*
                    Psalm 138:7

Jesus said,
*   "Do not let your hearts*
*   be troubled.*
*   Trust in God;*
*   trust also in me."*

*   "Peace I leave with you;*
*   my peace I give you.*
*   I do not give to you*
*   as the world gives.*
*   Do not let your hearts be troubled*
*   and do not be afraid."*
                    John 14:1, 27

*The Lord is close
to the
brokenhearted
and saves
those who are
crushed in
spirit.*

Psalm 34:18

*Cast all
your anxiety
on him
because
he cares
for you.*

1 Peter 5:7

Mistrust

You may be wondering
    if there is anyone
        you can really trust.

Is there anyone
    who will not betray you,
        or fail you?

Your wife? or
    Your husband?

        Your attorney?

        The Judge?

        Friends?

Is there anyone
    you can trust completely?

        Yes!

God will not leave you.
    He will not fail you
        or betray you.

He will stand by you no matter what.

    Trust Him.

The Bible says . . .

Because of the Lord's great love
*   we are not consumed,*
for his compassions never fail.
They are new every morning;
*   great is your faithfulness.*

                    Lamentations 3:22–23

Trust in the Lord
*   with all your heart*
and lean not
*   on your own understanding;*
in all your ways acknowledge him,
*   and he will make*
*   your paths straight.*

                        Proverbs 3:5–6

Those who know your name
*   will trust in you,*
for you, Lord,
*   have never forsaken*
*   those who seek you.*

                        Psalm 9:10

I trust in your
*   unfailing love;*
my heart rejoices
*   in your salvation.*

                        Psalm 13:5

Anger

When you hurt,
   you become angry
      with the people and things
         that cause you pain...

Angry at the System
   which treats you like a
      Non-person.

Angry at yourself
   for getting into this mess.

Angry at God for allowing this to happen.

Unresolved anger
   fills you with bitterness
      and controls you.

Let God control your anger.

Let Him take it away.

Simply ask,
   and He will help you
      find peace with yourself
         and others.

Let God provide you with a
   Holy Spirit-controlled
      temper.

The Bible says . . .

My dear brothers, take note of this:
Everyone should be quick to listen,
slow to speak
and slow to become angry,
for man's anger does not bring about
the righteous life
that God desires.

James 1:19-20

A patient man has great
understanding,
but a quick-tempered man
displays folly.

Proverbs 14:29

A gentle answer turns away wrath,
but a harsh word
stirs up anger.

Proverbs 15:1

Refrain from anger and turn from wrath;
do not fret —
it leads only to evil.

Psalm 37:8

"In your anger do not sin:"
Do not let the sun go down
while you are still angry,
and do not give the devil
a foothold.

Ephesians 4:26-27

Hatred

Hatred nourishes itself.

The more you think
     about your enemies
     and the wrongs they have done you,
          the angrier you become.

Filled with bitterness,
     unhappy,
     and
consumed with thoughts of revenge,
     you are trapped.

Just like Satan, the captor,
     wants you to be.

But God wants to free you from this trap.

Because God is love.

His love can come into your life
and loose you from these
     bitter feelings of
          hatred and resentment.

And His love can fill your mind
     with the good things of God.

His love can become your love.

The Bible says . . .

Jesus said,
"A new command I give you:
Love one another.
As I have loved you,
so you must love one another."

John 13:34

Get rid of all bitterness, rage and anger,
brawling and slander,
along with every form of malice.
Be kind and compassionate to one another,
forgiving each other,
just as in Christ God forgave you.

Ephesians 4:31-32

Jesus said,
"...Love your enemies
and pray for those
who persecute you,
that you may be sons
of your Father
in heaven."

Matthew 5:44-45

For if you forgive men
when they sin against you,
your heavenly Father
will also forgive you.

Matthew 6:14

Can love grow
in the midst
of opposition,
bitterness,
and hatred?

It can—
if it is
<u>God's</u> love!

Loneliness

You know what it is to be lonely.

Isolated from family,
Cut off from friends, and
    thrown into a world where
    no one seems to care,
You are left
empty and scared.

But you can't be locked away from God.

There's no place in the universe
    that God can't go with you.

No one,
No thing,
No force
    in heaven or earth
        can separate you from God.

God cares for you.

He won't leave you alone.

He promised.

The Bible says . . .

God is our refuge and strength,
   an ever-present help
     in trouble.

Psalm 46:1

...God has said,
   "Never will I leave you;
   never will I forsake you."

Hebrews 13:5

Who shall separate us
   from the love of Christ?
Shall trouble or hardship
   or persecution or famine
   or nakedness or danger or sword?
...No, in all these things
   we are more than conquerors
   through him who loved us.

Romans 8:35-37

So do not fear,
   for I am with you;
do not be dismayed,
   for I am your God.
I will strengthen you
   and help you;
I will uphold you
   with my righteous right hand.

Isaiah 41:10

Separation from family —

Jesus understands what it is like
    for you to be separated
    from your family.

Your support system is cut
    like His was
    on the cross...

His Heavenly Father was still there.
    Somewhere.
    But when He cried out,
    "Why have you forsaken me?"
    There was no answer.

His mother was still there.
    Somewhere.
But she couldn't help Him.

His family was still there.
    Somewhere.
But they were separated.

That's why He understands
    what it is like
for you to be separated
    from your family.
And that's why He made it possible
    for you to be born
    into His family.
And that's why He promised
    never to leave you alone.
    Not even once!

The Bible says . . .

Though my father and mother
    forsake me,
the Lord will receive me.

Psalm 27:10

The Spirit himself testifies
    with our spirit
that we are God's children.

Romans 8:16

...Be strong and courageous.
    Do not be terrified;
    do not be discouraged,
for the Lord your God
    will be with you
    wherever you go.

Joshua 1:9

The Lord himself goes before you
    and will be with you;
he will never leave you
    nor forsake you.

Deuteronomy 31:8

Captive

Everyone has been imprisoned sometime.

Perhaps you have been
   taken captive, too,
   in a way that you
      didn't even know about.

Satan is the captor.
He wants you to be
   bound
   and shackled.
He guards you jealously.

Only God has the key that can
   set you free.

   Jesus.

Jesus was taken captive, too.
   Not by the Romans
      or by the Jews.
   Not even by Satan himself.

   But by our sins.

He died for our sins.
   And then He rose from the grave
   and defeated
      death
      and Satan
   for your Freedom.

Now you can be truly free!

The Bible says . . .

...All have sinned and fall short
of the glory of God....

Romans 3:23

The wages of sin is death,
but the gift of God
is eternal life in Christ Jesus
our Lord.

Romans 6:23

Jesus said,
"The Spirit of the Lord
is on me...
to preach good news
to the poor.
He has sent me to proclaim freedom
for the prisoners
and recovery of sight
for the blind,
to release the oppressed,
to proclaim the year
of the Lord's favor."

Luke 4:18–19

So if the Son [Jesus] sets you free,
you will be free indeed.

John 8:36

*If the Son [Jesus]
    sets you free,
    you will
    be free
    indeed.*

                        John 8:36

Therefore,
  there is now
  no condemnation
  for those
  who are in
  Christ Jesus.

                    Romans 8:1

Guilt

"Guilty!" pronounces the judge.
"Guilty!" shouts society.
"Guilty!" echoes your conscience.

When you think about your sins,
    you are loaded down
    with heavy feelings of guilt.
And you wonder if God could possibly
    forgive you
    and remove this burden
    of guilt.

            He can!

No matter what you've done,
    God can forgive you.

    Not only that,
    He wants to forgive you.

Tell Him how sorry you are
    for what you have done,
And ask Him to take away
    your guilt and your sin.

When you sincerely confess your sin
    and trust in Jesus
    to save you,
All your sins will be forgiven
    and you won't have
    to feel guilty anymore.
Ever!

The Bible says . . .

If we confess our sins,
*   he is faithful and just*
*   and will forgive us our sins*
*   and purify us*
*   from all unrighteousness.*

1 John 1:9

Who is a God like you,
*   who pardons sin...?*
You do not stay angry forever
*   but delight to show mercy.*
You will again have compassion
*   on us;*
You will tread our sins underfoot
*   and hurl all our iniquities*
*   into the depths of the sea.*

Micah 7:18-19

As far as the east
*   is from the west,*
so far has he removed
*   our transgressions from us.*

Psalm 103:12

Therefore, there is now no condemnation
*   for those who are*
*   in Christ Jesus....*

Romans 8:1

Repentance

There may be things in your past
    you would like
        to change,
people you would like
        to apologize to,
    or mistakes you would like
        to undo.
There may be many things
    you would like to do over
        if you could,
    but you can't.
You cannot change the past.

But God can change YOU.

Every one of your past sins
    can be taken away
    if you are truly sorry for them.
Ask God to forgive you.
    Ask Jesus to come
        into your heart.
Not only will He
    clean up your past,
but He will help you
    to stay clean.
Today,
    Tomorrow,
        and Always!

The Bible says . . .

After I strayed,
*   I repented;*
after I came to understand,
I beat my breast.
I was ashamed and humiliated
*   because I bore the disgrace*
*   of my youth.*

                                    Jeremiah 31:19

Have mercy on me, O God,
*   according to your unfailing love;*
according to your great compassion
*   blot out my transgressions.*
Wash away all my iniquity
*   and cleanse me from my sin.*

                                    Psalm 51:1-2

The Lord is compassionate and gracious,
*   slow to anger,*
*   abounding in love.*
...He does not treat us
*   as our sins deserve*
or repay us according
*   to our iniquities.*

                                    Psalm 103:8-10

...Though your sins are like scarlet,
*   they shall be as white as snow;*
though they are red as crimson,
*   they shall be like wool.*

                                    Isaiah 1:18

Paid in full

When Jesus died on the cross,
   He gave God a receipt
   with the names of all the believers
     on it.
The receipt is clearly marked:
   "Penalties for all sins
    PAID IN FULL."

The debt is paid,
   and the debtors forgiven.

Sometimes it's hard to believe
   that someone would
   do that for you.

You know you owe the debt,
   and you wonder
   what the catch is.

But there is no catch.
   God's offer is on the level.

All you have to do
   is repent and believe
and then accept
   this wonderful gift from
   a wonderful Father.

The Bible says . . .

For God so loved the world
that he gave
his one and only Son,
that whoever believes in him
shall not perish
but have eternal life.
For God did not send his Son
into the world
to condemn the world,
but to save the world through him.

John 3:16-17

He [Jesus] was pierced
for our transgressions,
he was crushed
for our iniquities;
the punishment that brought us peace
was upon him,
and by his wounds
we are healed.

Isaiah 53:5

We all, like sheep,
have gone astray,
each of us has turned
to his own way;
and the Lord has laid on him
the iniquity of us all.

Isaiah 53:6

He who conceals
his sins
does not prosper,
but whoever confesses
and renounces them
finds mercy.

Proverbs 28:13

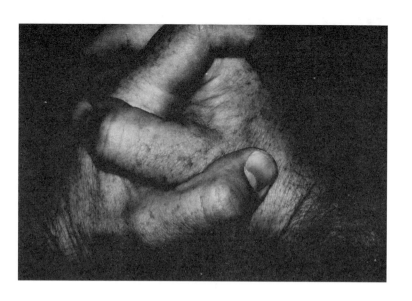

I acknowledged my sin
        to you
        and did not
        cover up
        my iniquity.
I said, "I will confess
        my transgressions
        to the Lord"—
        and you forgave
        the guilt
        of my sin.

                        Psalm 32:5

Pardoned

One of the most wonderful things
about God
is that even though
He knows your sins
and offenses,
He still loves you enough
to forgive you.

God has a full pardon ready
to grant you
when you ask for it
in repentance
and faith.

He sent His Son to pay for it,
His Word to tell you about it,
and
His Spirit to deliver it.

His forgiveness is complete
and unconditional
to those who will
receive it
in faith.

God's love for you is so
wonderful
that your request
for forgiveness
can never exceed
His supply of love
to grant it!

The Bible says . . .

Whoever believes in him [Jesus]
*   is not condemned,*
but whoever does not believe
*   stands condemned already*
*   because he has not believed*
in the name of God's one and only Son.

John 3:18

Let the wicked forsake his way
*   and the evil man his thoughts.*
Let him turn to the Lord,
*   and he will have mercy*
*   on him,*
and to our God,
*   for he will freely*
*   pardon.*

Isaiah 55:7

Blessed is he whose transgressions
*   are forgiven,*
*   whose sins are covered.*
Blessed is the man
*   whose sin*
*   the Lord does not count*
*   against him*
and in whose spirit
*   is no deceit.*

Psalm 32:1-2

The Enemy

Satan is God's enemy
    and he is your enemy.

Satan knows he cannot attack God
    directly
    so he sends demons
        to attack God's creation
        which you are a part of.

The ministry of demons is to
    harass,
        tempt,
            and afflict you.

Satan wants to put you
    into his trick-bag.

Now for the last 2000 years
    God has provided armor
        against the wicked one.

Full protection is yours as you put on the
    armor of God in Power
        and Strength
        and Might.

Now instead of being the Victim
    you
        can
            be the Victor!

The Bible says . . .

Be strong in the Lord
   and in his mighty power.
Put on the full armor of God
   so that you can take your stand
   against the devil's schemes.
For our struggle is not
   against flesh and blood, but...
   against the powers of this dark world....
Therefore put on the full armor of God,
   so that when the day of evil comes,
   you may be able to stand your ground....
Stand firm then, with the belt of truth
   buckled around your waist,
   with the breastplate of righteousness
      in place,
   and with your feet fitted
      with the readiness that comes
      from the gospel of peace.
In addition to all this,
   take up the shield of faith,
   with which you can extinguish
      all the flaming arrows
      of the evil one.
Take the helmet of salvation
   and the sword of the Spirit,
   which is the word of God.
And pray in the Spirit on all occasions
   with all kinds of prayers and requests.
                              Ephesians 6:10-18

Fear

Jesus knows what it is like
    to be afraid.
He knew that His last few days on earth
    would be filled
    with many trials
        and hardships.
He knew the cross awaited Him.

He even asked God
    to take away His suffering
        if possible.

But going to the cross
    was the only way
    to free you from your bondage.
So he accepted God's will.

Jesus was able to look beyond
    what man had in store for Him
    to the peace that awaited Him
        from God His Father.

He can help you
    through your trials
        and hardships.

And when you are afraid,
    He will help you
    and guide you beyond
to the place God has
    especially for you.

The Bible says . . .

Be strong and courageous.
Do not be afraid
or terrified . . .
for the Lord your God goes with you;
he will never leave you
nor forsake you.

Deuteronomy 31:6

The Lord is my light
and my salvation—
whom shall I fear?
The Lord is the stronghold
of my life—
of whom shall I be afraid?

Psalm 27:1

Are not five sparrows sold
for two pennies?
Yet not one of them is forgotten
by God.
Indeed, the very hairs of your head
are all numbered.
Don't be afraid;
you are worth more
than many sparrows.

Luke 12:6-7

In God I trust;
I will not be afraid.
What can man do to me?

Psalm 56:11

Patience

When you are no longer
     in control of your life,
and every detail of your existence
     depends solely on the decisions of others,
you become anxious
                    restless
                    impatient.

Waiting for letters and visitors,
     for decisions from courts
          or parole boards,
     or just waiting for nothing
          in particular.

Waiting for men.
Waiting for God.

Why does God allow you
     to face all these frustrations?

Perhaps to teach you patience,
     or to learn to depend on Him,
or to give you time
     to seek Him out,
     to study His Word,
     to really get to know Him.

Tell Him what you need,
     and then wait with
     patience, expectation, and assurance.

God will surely hear your prayers.

The Bible says . . .

We wait in hope
*   for the Lord;*
he is our help
*   and our shield.*

May your unfailing love
*   rest upon us,*
*   O Lord,*
*   even as we put*
*   our hope*
*   in you.*

Psalm 33:20-22

I waited patiently
*   for the Lord;*
he turned to me
*   and heard my cry.*
He lifted me
*   out of the slimy pit,*
*   out of the mud*
*   and mire;*
he set my feet
*   on a rock*
*   and gave me*
*   a firm place*
*   to stand.*

Psalm 40:1-2

Those who hope
   in the Lord
   will renew
   their strength.
They will soar
   on wings
   like eagles;
they will run
   and not
   grow weary,
they will walk
   and not
   be faint.

Isaiah 40:31

Prayer

Sometimes you may wonder
   if God has abandoned you,
when all the time
   He is by your side
   waiting for you to call
   on Him in prayer.

Prayer is just talking with God.

It is a special gift from God to you.

Prayer can help you find direction
   in your life. And give you...
      Comfort in the midst of sorrow.
      Peace in the midst of turmoil.
      Stability in the midst of change.
      Forgiveness in the midst of sin.
      Love in the midst of hate.

Through prayer you make yourself
   available to God.

Talking with God may feel awkward
   at first,
but rest assured that He
   hears and understands.
And soon prayer will become
   your lifeline.

Don't neglect this wonderful gift
   from God.

The Bible says . . .

The Lord is near to all
    who call on him,
to all who call on him
    in truth.

                Psalm 145:18

This is the confidence we have
    in approaching God:
that if we ask anything
    according to his will,
        he hears us.

                1 John 5:14

Ask and it will be given
    to you;
seek and you will find;
knock and the door will be opened
    to you.
For everyone who asks receives;
    he who seeks finds;
    and to him who knocks,
        the door will be opened.

                Matthew 7:7–8

Let us then approach
    the throne of grace
        with confidence,
so that we may receive mercy
    and find grace to help us
        in our time of need.

                Hebrews 4:16

Invitation

You can know true freedom when you know Jesus Christ. Here are four steps to begin or maintain a relationship with Him:

1. **Read the Bible—every day!**
    God wrote the Bible for you. Spend time listening to what He has to say.

2. **Talk to God—every day.**
    God is here, right now, ready to listen. Just tell Him what's on your mind. If you want the gift of salvation and don't know what to say, simply and sincerely pray: *Dear God, I confess that I am a sinner who needs your forgiveness. I am truly sorry for my sins and want to forsake them and flee from them. Please forgive me. I believe that Jesus died on the cross to pay the penalty for my sins, and that He rose again from the dead for my salvation. I accept Him as my Savior and promise to follow Him as my Lord. Thank you, Father, for your wonderful love. In Jesus' name. Amen.*

3. **Keep it up.**
    It can be hard, but it's important to keep reading the Bible and praying.

4. **Let others know.**
    As you begin to experience freedom in Jesus Christ, share with others how talking and listening to God has helped you.

The Bible says . . .

If you confess with your mouth,
"Jesus is Lord"
and believe in your heart
that God raised him
from the dead,
you will be saved.
For it is with your heart
that you believe
and are justified,
and it is with your mouth
that you confess
and are saved.

Romans 10:9-10

Because of his great love for us,
God, who is rich in mercy,
made us alive with Christ
even when we were dead
in transgressions—
it is by grace you have been saved.

Ephesians 2:4-5

To all who received him [Jesus],
to those who believed
in his name,
he gave the right to become
children of God....

John 1:12

Welcome to the Family of God!

Titles in the **Friendship Series** include:

*A Miracle of Love**
A Promise of Life
As Real As You
Back to Wholeness
*Full Pardon**
*God Understands**
Living Long and Loving It!
Love that Lasts
Never Alone
Never too Late
*Someone Cares**
Stress: letting go and letting God
Talking with God
Who Cares When I Hurt?

* Also available in Spanish

This booklet has been given to you by

**Contact us if you need further help in learning
how to live and walk with God.**